Dr. Emmanuel Rotimi Onabanjo
Pastor/Divine Servant PAE Ministry

THE YOKE BREAKER

Be set free from Yokes, be set up for Glory by applying 31 days of devil-demolishing declarations

THE YOKE BREAKER

© 2016 by Emmanuel Rotimi Onabanjo

All rights reserved. No part of this booklet may be reproduced or transmitted in any form or by any means without permission in writing from the author, except brief quotations used in critical articles or reviews.

Scripture quotations taken from the King James Version (KJV)

Printed in the United States of America

INTRODUCTION

The Epistle of James 1:2-7 states: "My brethren, count it all joy when ye fall into divers temptations; knowing this, that the trying of your faith worketh patience. But let patience have her perfect work, that ye may be perfect and entire, wanting nothing. If any of you lack wisdom, let him ask of God, that giveth to all men liberally, and upbraideth not; and it shall be given him. But let him ask in faith, nothing wavering. For he that wavereth is like a wave of the sea driven with the wind and tossed. For let not that man think that he shall receive any thing of the Lord" Beloved, I congratulate you for being led to lay hands on this book. You have in your hands a mighty covenant of grace and renewal. Before you start reading the chapters, note that your fate depends on your FAITH. This book will work as you release your faith over your desires. The Holy Spirit directed me to write this book of prayers, in order to reveal the Lord's power through the pages of a unique medium. To confirm the uniqueness of the book, gently place it close to your chest; close your eyes briefly, say Amen seven times, and see what happens in your spirit. I guarantee you that this book will break every yoke, and lead you to desired heights in the name of Jesus Christ. Read each chapter daily, including the suggested scriptures. For the months without 31 days, read additional chapters on the last day of those months. Be very expectant, and move by faith. Do not doubt whatever God places in your mind once you start using this book. I pray that your praise report will be the greatest and fastest to get to me. Finally, help others by sending copies to them, and let me hear from you. Be blessed and highly favored, in the name of Jesus Christ, Amen.

Pastor Emmanuel Rotimi Onabanjo

DAY ONE

Empowered for Success

TODAY I begin the season of a fresh covenant of Amazing Heights and Peace. The Spirit of the Lord is upon me, and I am being led by divine wisdom. No chain shall be able to hold me. No plot shall stop me from a victorious path. By

the Spirit of the Lord, I shall run through a troop and subdue groups of adversaries. This day, I am empowered for success. This day, I will fulfill my expectations. This day, favor will flow all around me. I have been qualified for quality expansion. Love and grace are all over my day. I decree and declare over this day: BE BLESSED FOR MY SAKE; the spirit of the Lord goes with me. Today, I command and receive liberty. I am a celebrity for God's Kingdom. I declare it, I believe it and it is SETTLED in the name of Jesus Christ, Amen.

SCRIPTURES

2 Corinthians 1:7
And our hope of you is stedfast, knowing, that as ye are partakers of the sufferings, so shall ye be also of the consolation.

Isaiah 60:1
Arise, shine; for thy light is come, and the glory of the LORD is risen upon thee.

Psalm 18:29
For by thee I have run through a troop; and by my God have I leaped over a wall.

DAY TWO

Audacity of Success

TODAY I (your name here) decree and declare that the Spirit and audacity of success are all over me. The Lord has delivered me from the strivings of haters and mockers. Both strangers and those familiar to me shall serve me, according to the purpose of increase that the Lord has sent over my day.

Today is not like any other day. This is my day of approval. No delay tactics will taint my day. No evil plot will survive beyond the coast of the plotters. Haters shall not mock me. Every mouth of the enemy is hereby stopped. I shall relish in my peace, as the Almighty God fights my battle. The Lord has declared me blessed; therefore, I command every creation of God to stand still, till I achieve everything that the Lord has promised me. I call forth rain and riches. I call forth promotion and expansion. I call forth uncommon favor. Today my head is anointed with the oil of gladness; therefore, my day shall end on a note of jubilation. I declare it, I believe it and it is settled, in the name of Jesus Christ, Amen.

SCRIPTURES

2 Samuel 22:44
44 Thou also hast delivered me from the strivings of my people, thou hast kept me to be head of the heathen: a people which I knew not shall serve me.

Psalm 63:11
11 But the king shall rejoice in God; every one that sweareth by him shall glory: but the mouth of them that speak lies shall be stopped.

Deuteronomy 11:14
14 That I will give you the rain of your land in his due season, the first rain and the latter rain, that thou mayest gather in thy corn, and thy wine, and thine oil.

Judges 6:14-15 (*Gideon Becomes Israel's Judge*)

DAY THREE

Comforted in the Lord

TODAY I (your name) decree and declare that I am being rewarded. Greater and mightier rewards are locating me in the name of Jesus Christ. I give thanks to God for the favor upon my home and my loved ones. We have a good God.

His kindness shall bring us to our coast of increase, and we shall dwell in safety and comfort. No man shall overpower us as we confront and subdue blockers of missions. We have been declared Winners, and the battle is won. No more dispossessions. We possess our divine portion, and our goodness is sealed by the blood of Jesus Christ. Now, this day, I command over you, according to the power that works in me, bring forth the abundance of nations into my home. Let nations serve me. Let the earth respect my intentions. Let the mighty come to me for counsel. I shall be led by the Lord. My portion is great. My day is fruitful. My efforts shall never end in desolation. I step out in determination; I shall return in celebration. SETTLED, IN THE NAME OF JESUS CHRIST.

SCRIPTURES

Isaiah 61:7
7 For your shame ye shall have double; and for confusion they shall rejoice in their portion: therefore in their land they shall possess the double: everlasting joy shall be unto them.

Deuteronomy 11: 23-25 *(Loving and Obeying God)*

THE YOKE BREAKER

DAY FOUR

Peace during Distress

TODAY I (your name) decree and declare, I am not forgotten. My hopes are not dashed. I am not forsaken. My aspirations are becoming manifestations. My home is peaceful. My room is anointed with graceful approval.

None shall make me angry. I will not yield to distractions. Evil tongues shall not prevail over my day. The Lord is fully in charge of my mind. I am not losing my mind to evil forces. I am not bowing to thoughts of depression. I command peace, and I have peace. I command joy and it is locating me by the flood. Instead of disgrace, I have grace for mighty exploits. Instead of sorrow, I have super gladness. Every form of blockage, I surrender you to the mighty hands of God. Nothing shall stop me today. I am not truncated but accelerated. I am not depressed but empowered. I am not negotiating my destiny away from fruition. I am an achiever, I will achieve the purpose of God in my life: my health, my wealth and my strength, I command you to react favorably to my destiny. I am a champion, and I will not settle for less. I am stepping out today into approval, increase and divine exploits. Devil, get off my path. I have awesome work to do for the Lord. No destruction. No obstruction. I am determined to fulfill my day, and it shall be well, in the name of Jesus Christ, Amen.

SCRIPTURES

Isaiah 54:17
17 No weapon that is formed against thee shall prosper; and every tongue that shall rise against thee in judgment thou shalt condemn. This is the heritage of the servants of the LORD, and their righteousness is of me, saith the LORD.

Psalm 18:39-40
39 For thou hast girded me with strength unto the battle: thou hast subdued under me those that rose up against me. 40 Thou hast also given me the necks of mine enemies; that I might destroy them that hate me.

Psalm 25:2
2 O my God, I trust in thee: let me not be ashamed, let not mine enemies triumph over me.

DAY FIVE

God's Sustaining Power

TODAY I declare that no evil shall come near me and my entire loved ones. No pestilence shall invade my dwelling, and I am delivered from every plague and protected from every ill wind. I am the beloved of the Lord; I am loved

perfectly by a perfect God. All fear is defeated and my tomorrow is secure because He holds my future, my life is worth living. I will attain unto the fullness of purpose; my destiny will not be truncated, and I will not be stranded. I am on the Lord's side, His ears are open to my cry, and He will receive my sacrifices; my offerings are accepted. My seed is in good ground and my harvest is sure. I will not be rejected. I REBUKE AND REJECT DEPRESSION. I AM NOT HAVING IT. This is my year of super increase. My family dwells in the secret place of God. We are safe forever. I am established in His favor. I am protected: God fights my battles, and I hold my peace, in Jesus' name. I believe and I say Amen.

SCRIPTURES

Ephesians 1:6
6 To the praise of the glory of his grace, wherein he hath made us accepted in the beloved.

Luke 8:8
8 And other fell on good ground, and sprang up, and bare fruit an hundredfold. And when he had said these things, he cried, He that hath ears to hear, let him hear.

Psalm 72:12
12 For he shall deliver the needy when he crieth; the poor also, and him that hath no helper.

Isaiah 51:9-11, (The Lord Comforts Zion)
Psalm 55: 1-9 (The LORD Will Sustain)
Isaiah 54:4-7 (Blessings through the Servant)

DAY SIX

Unstoppable Journey to Greatness

IN the name of Jesus Christ, I decree and declare that God is the Champion of my journey. He leads me along the path of righteousness. My journey to greatness is unstoppable. I refuse to be a loser. I refuse to beg for bread. I refuse to negotiate with

principalities in dark places. I shall tread my enemies to the earth, they shall be silent in shallow graves. My horn is exalted today. As I seek, I will find. As I knock, doors of opportunities will open. I receive mighty fulfillment. This is my day of grace. The oil of joy shall fill my life. I HAVE DIVINE MANDATE FOR HIGHER GROUNDS. NO DEVIL CAN STOP ME. Now, every creation of God, start locating me with gifts; honest assistance and endless love. I AM CHOSEN TO LIVE. DEATH YOU ARE DESTROYED. I have declared in faith, it shall be done speedily, in Jesus name, Amen.

SCRIPTURES

Deuteronomy 31:8
8 And the LORD, he it is that doth go before thee; he will be with thee, he will not fail thee, neither forsake thee: fear not, neither be dismayed.

Isaiah 45:2-3
2 I will go before thee, and make the crooked places straight: I will break in pieces the gates of brass, and cut in sunder the bars of iron: 3 And I will give thee the treasures of darkness, and hidden riches of secret places, that thou mayest know that I, the LORD, which call thee by thy name, am the God of Israel.

Psalm 37:28
28 For the LORD loveth judgment, and forsaketh not his saints; they are preserved for ever: but the seed of the wicked shall be cut off.

Exodus 23:27 *(God's Promise of Protection)*
Psalm 18:40 *(Calling upon God)*
2 Samuel 22:41 *(David's Praise for Deliverance)*
Jeremiah 1:12 *(The Prophet's Call)*

DAY SEVEN

Peace in God's Grace

TODAY I decree and declare that the Lord rejoices over me, and my expectations shall end in joy. The Lord is the lifter of my head, enemies shall not prevail over my aspirations. God has loved with his divine caring love; therefore, I will

forever be glad, not sad. My home is a citadel of grace; therefore, my future is secured with divine seal. Prosperity is my inheritance in Jesus Christ. I have endless supplies of rain and riches. Incantations of desperate evildoers cannot stop me. Arrows of destiny blockers cannot prevail in my direction. Plots of the devil shall return to the sender. Grace speaks for me. Faith lifts my countenance. I receive help from affliction and obstructions, my path is a sure path of success. My God loves me with passion. He cuddles me in his arms. No harm shall penetrate my home. My loved ones are under God's security. I am not losing anyone to untimely death. This is my season of advancement. This is my season of promotions. This is my season of elevation. This is my time to be rewarded. The creations of God shall bless me endlessly. Honor shall be poured over me endlessly. I am not useless; I am not depressed, I am not neglected. My days shall be filled with laughter. My blood shall speak of better days. I am the redeemed, not the forgotten. My glory, I call you forth in the name of Jesus; rise and accelerate to higher heights. It is my time to shine; it is my season of happiness. I declare these things, and they are settled in Jesus' name, Amen.

SCRIPTURES

Proverbs 10:28
28 *The hope of the righteous shall be gladness: but the expectation of the wicked shall perish.*

DAY EIGHT

A Season of Greatness

TODAY the Lord is releasing to me great treasures and pleasures. My life shall experience divine love in a new fashion. This day will favor me in all my aspirations. Every mouth against my destiny is hereby condemned. The accuser is cursed for my sake. Satan has lost the battle. I am a Winner. I am not the next candidate for the grave. I am next in line for mouth-gaping miracles. I am the beloved of the Lord. This day, God will order my steps into heights uncommon. This day, my health will agree with divine touch. Increase shall locate my door. Blessings shall men deposit at my door. I will be approved for promotion. Angels of God will deliver my good news. I am specially crafted; therefore, honor and respect shall accompany my day. This is my season of greatness, and no plot of evil shall be able to stop my destiny. I declare these things, and they shall appear as

declared in Jesus' name, Amen.

SCRIPTURES

Isaiah 54:17
17 No weapon that is formed against thee shall prosper; and every tongue that shall rise against thee in judgment thou shalt condemn. This is the heritage of the servants of the LORD, and their righteousness is of me, saith the LORD.

Jeremiah 33:6
6 Behold, I will bring it health and cure, and I will cure them, and will reveal unto them the abundance of peace and truth.

Psalm 119: 133
133 Order my steps in thy word: and let not any iniquity have dominion over me.

DAY NINE

Confidence in God's Sovereignty

TODAY I speak over my life and my household that the God of Abraham, Isaac and Jacob shall supply all our needs. I will not be frustrated before I am appointed for greater heights. My future is secure. Angelic host ministers to me.

I have divine assistance. I am receiving approval and assistance from the throne of God. My faith in the word of God is being rewarded. Favor speaks for me. Grace backs me up. I am divinely packaged and shielded from calamity. This day shall end on a note of joy. My reward shall not be meager, but mega. I will reap bountiful harvests. No hardships, no failure and no accident. God delights in me, so shall my days be filled with divine visitations. My brighter days are just beginning. Open heavens are my portion. I am an overcomer, blessed with all spiritual blessings. My foundation is solid. I fear no failure. I am ending today with signs: wonders and miracles. I declare these things, and they are approved and settled in Jesus' name, Amen.

SCRIPTURES

John 16:33
33 These things I have spoken unto you, that in me ye might have peace. In the world ye shall have tribulation: but be of good cheer; I have overcome the world.

Psalm 33:21
21 For our heart shall rejoice in him, because we have trusted in his holy name.

Romans 5:8
8 But God commendeth his love toward us, in that, while we were yet sinners, Christ died for us.

DAY TEN

Faith in God's Promises

TODAY I step out in faith, to achieve the miraculous. My season of favor and fulfilled promise is in full gear. My God is a promise keeper, and He shall make His word perfect over me. My God is the Way Maker and He is

turning obstacles to opportunities for me. My God is the Wisdom Giver, and He is ordering my steps according to His word. Jesus is my peace and my joy. I am being instructed to prosper. I receive excellent spirit, and I will stand out wherever I go this day. My God shall exceed my expectations and I will bless His name at all times. I speak against difficulties. They shall not discourage me to dump vital opportunities. People under demonic spirit of envy, anger and arguments shall be driven away from my path. The goodness of the Lord shall endure over me as long as the sun and moon exist. Today I am making progress. Today my ideas shall make sense. Today my efforts will attract rewards. I will return extremely happy and the Lord will rejoice over me with songs and dance. I declare these things, and no devil in hell shall be able to stop me, Amen.

SCRIPTURES

Psalm 16:10
10 For thou wilt not leave my soul in hell; neither wilt thou suffer thine Holy One to see corruption.

Isaiah 43:19
19 Behold, I will do a new thing; now it shall spring forth; shall ye not know it? I will even make a way in the wilderness, and rivers in the desert.

THE YOKE BREAKER

DAY ELEVEN

Free-flowing Grace

TODAY is my day of rain and riches. Wealth of nations are being assigned to locate me. This is the covenant of the Lord upon me and my home. God is fulfilling my petitions. God is having compassion over my offering. God is defending us with a mighty host of Angels. Joy unspeakable. Celebrations unstoppable. Lofty heights are the rewards of my efforts. My God is honoring me today. I will be greatly enhanced for optimal performance. My eyes shall see better days, and the treasures of God shall heed my call. Rivers of free-flowing grace are approved to bring me desired abundance. The Lord has washed me clean, I am qualified to be beautified. I am purified to be edified. I am chosen to be honored. My hopes shall not suffer abortion. I am in super progress, advancing without obstructions. My path is clear. I am unhindered for greater heights. This day will bless me. This day will fill me with divinely selected grains. I am ending without blemish. Nothing excellent will elude me. I am under a divine covering. My glory, RISE AND SHINE, in the name of THE YOKE BREAKER, Amen.

SCRIPTURES

Deuteronomy 11:14
14 That I will give you the rain of your land in his due season, the first rain and the latter rain, that thou mayest gather in thy corn, and thy wine, and thine oil.

Deuteronomy 28:6
6 Blessed shalt thou be when thou comest in, and blessed shalt thou be when thou goest out.

Genesis 12:2
2 And I will make of thee a great nation, and I will bless thee, and make thy name great; and thou shalt be a blessing:

Psalm 37:25 *(Grace to the Righteous)*
Zephaniah 3:17 (Jerusalem's Redemption)

DAY TWELVE

Abundance of Favor

TODAY the God of abundance and favor has declared me chosen for greatness. I am a fruitful bough by a well of supplies. My branches are spreading beyond human comprehension. The Lord has given me wisdom beyond my challenges. I will make excellent grades today and always. I speak divine security over me and my loved ones, no arrow of the enemy shall find our domain. As I step out today, the mighty strength of the Lord shall move me into the heights of global prominence. I shall be known as a well-nourished, divinely positioned child of the most high Jehovah. No plan of the enemy shall be able to destabilize me. I rise beyond the plots of limitations. I am focused on beauty and increase, and they shall locate me. The name of Jesus Christ is going before me, and making every crooked path straight. I am not approaching my day in fear. I am walking and tackling things by faith. I have great understanding, and I decree the excellence of God to favor my path. I pray these things, and I

believe they are settled, in the name of Jesus Christ, Amen.

SCRIPTURES

Genesis 49:22, Exodus 33:15.

Genesis 49:22
22 Joseph is a fruitful bough, even a fruitful bough by a well; whose branches run over the wall:

Exodus 33:15
15 And he said unto him, If thy presence go not with me, carry us not up hence.

THE YOKE BREAKER

DAY THIRTEEN

Anointing of Excellence

TODAY I speak good works over me and over the lives of my loved ones. Today I overcome every obstacles of the enemy, and I soar like an eagle. I am rising from glory to glory. I am an achiever. I am unstoppable and the gates of

hell are disgraced for my sake. My future is secured. My destiny is open and inviting. My progress in life is certain and I have access to eternal prosperity. Through Jesus Christ, my inheritance is reserved and sealed under a divine covenant. The anointing of excellence is all over me. The power for perfection lives inside of me. Evil is put behind me. Success is my portion. The hands of grace are lifting me away from hostilities. My trip is blessed and safe. I am not a partaker of sorrow. I have my petition answered. Every tongue shall speak of glory of the Lord over me. The tongues of haters shall be stopped. My victory is certain. I am walking into favor and surplus. I declare these things; I believe them, and they shall be, according to my desires, in the name of Jesus Christ, Amen.

SCRIPTURES

Isaiah 45:19
19 I have not spoken in secret, in a dark place of the earth: I said not unto the seed of Jacob, Seek ye me in vain: I the LORD speak righteousness, I declare things that are right.

Psalm 1 *(The Way of the Righteous)*

DAY FOURTEEN

Promise of Everlasting Joy

TODAY I speak over me and over the lives of my loved ones, that we are shinning brighter and being elevated to heights of divine perfection. We have peace in all areas, and God has delivered us from the insurrection of destiny blockers.

We shall be fulfilled and not frustrated. We shall be rewarded, and not disappointed. We shall be promoted and not demoted. Heaven supports us wherever we go. I am the beloved of the Lord; therefore, I connect to power and authority for exploits. My place of super prosperity is affirmed. I am unshaken by hostilities, for the Lord is fighting my battle. There is a supernatural release upon me and my days just got approved for unquenchable happiness. I will not end up broke. I will not end up in disaster. I will fulfill purpose in comfort and my latter days shall be amazingly blessed. My generations shall be blessed through the favor upon me, and the generations of the righteous shall call me blessed. I have what I desire, I enjoy divine approval. My days are blessed and my body organs are blessed. No sorrow, no calamity in my home, in the name of Jesus Christ, Amen.

SCRIPTURES

Psalm 138.8
8 The LORD will perfect that which concerneth me: thy mercy, O LORD, endureth for ever: forsake not the works of thine own hands.

Psalm 7:1
1 O LORD my God, in thee do I put my trust: save me from all them that persecute me, and deliver me:

Isaiah 61:7
7 For your shame ye shall have double; and for confusion they shall rejoice in their portion: therefore in their land they shall possess the double: everlasting joy shall be unto them.

THE YOKE BREAKER

DAY FIFTEEN

Restored in the Spirit

THIS is my day of POWER. The benefits of God is toward my life. I find grace as I step out. Nothing is lost. I am restored in my spirit, body and soul. I receive knowledge to do the miraculous. No yoke is holding me further. The

might of the Lord is moving me to greater levels. My days are perfect, my health is perfect. Nothing is missing; nothing is broken. Curses shall head back to the senders, because my Lord has declared me blessed. No sin will speak denial toward me, because I have the righteousness of God through my Savior, Jesus Christ. Everyone will invest in me today. Everyone will respect me today. Every territory shall bow to the God that I serve, and they shall bring gifts to bless my life. My children will be commanders of increase. Their portions are blessed with all spiritual blessings. I am expecting uncommon blessings and having them in abundance. I declare peace in my bosom and peace in my relationship. Deceivers shall not prevail over my virtue. I have been packaged wonderfully and carefully. All things are working for good in my direction. I step out today; the best in this day shall locate me. I decree these things, and they shall be, in the name of Jesus Christ, Amen.

SCRIPTURES

Hebrews 8:12
12 For I will be merciful to their unrighteousness, and their sins and their iniquities will I remember no more.

Isaiah 43:25
I, even I, am he that blotteth out thy transgressions for mine own sake, and will not remember thy sins.

Deuteronomy 30:3-5 (A Call to Return to God)

DAY SIXTEEN

Supplying All My Need

TODAY I decree and declare that my needs are supplied, and my intentions are not ending in frustration. Goodness and mercy shall follow me and laughter of glory shall end my decisions. The Lord has approved me in advance; therefore, I step out in courage to ask and be rewarded. Nothing will stop me from attaining my purpose. My rewards are approaching in great numbers and they are exceedingly great. I am not expecting defeats, and none shall be in the way. I am expecting a brighter future, and that is settled by grace. I am of God, therefore I have overcome those obstacles in any form. The loving kindness of the Lord is toward me; therefore, I am secured to be unmoved by recession or depression. The Lord's countenance is lifted upon me. I have peace over haters and destroyers. No demon shall creep into my home, because the Lord has declared by habitation as a citadel of peace. I am free from hurt. I am free from sorrow. Enemies are put to shame. Today I am advancing despite the opposition. Every challenge, I turn it over to the Lord. I see victory; I speak victory, and I am ending victorious in the name of Jesus Christ, SETTLED.

SCRIPTURES

Philippians 4:19
19 But my God shall supply all your need according to his riches in glory by Christ Jesus.

Psalm 91 (The Security of the Godly)

DAY SEVENTEEN

Blessed in Faith and Favor

LORD Jesus, I thank you for this day. This shall be my day of approval over every desired lofty height. Nothing shall be able to stop my rising and shinning. My best days are ahead and I am approved by my deliverer. I am supernaturally blessed. Blessed in every area of endeavor and increasing in faith and favor. Death and sin have no dominion over me; therefore, I am not living in fear. My home is the habitation of the supernatural. I live under the lovingkindness of the Lord. My provision is divine, all things work for my good. I expect no blemish. I expect no rebuke. I will not fail. I will not fall. Every expectation of haters over my life is hereby put to shame. Those waiting for my days of calamity will die waiting, for they shall not witness me being put to shame. I am forgiven and accepted of the Lord. My glory is shinning, and my horn is lifted daily. I shall never be put to shame. Doors locked are being opened. Territories are opening. My advancement is determined and affirmed. No devilish agent shall pluck me off the street. I am protected. I am in the will of God. His banner is all over me. My trips are safe. My roof is intact. Today my Lord shall supply all my needs according to His riches in glory by Christ Jesus. I declare these things and I receive them as I step out, in the name of Jesus Christ, Amen.

SCRIPTURES

Isaiah 54:1-12 (Blessings through the Servant)

1 Sing, O barren, thou that didst not bear; break forth into singing, and cry aloud, thou that didst not travail with child: for more are the children of the desolate than the children of the married wife, saith the LORD. ...

THE YOKE BREAKER

DAY EIGHTEEN

Lifted and Gifted

TODAY I decree and declare that My season of glamor is There. The Lord is making a way for me out of the wilderness of fear and despair. Days of waiting in vain are over. Days of crying myself to sleep are over. Days of lack are over.

Days of loneliness are over. Days of neglect are over. Days of spiritual dryness are over. Days of incarceration are over. Days of being penniless are over. Days of weaknesses are over. Days of dryness are over. Days of worry are over. Days of pains are over. Days of unholy addictions are over. Days of gloominess are over. Days of associations with lying tongues and deceptive spirits are over. My haters are demolished. My mockers are silenced. My adversaries are swallowed in shame. I have freedom from demonic rapists. My dreams are now clear. My vision is sanctified to fly. My mission is now in the flight of possibilities. I will not end my destiny in the trash can. Heaven supports me. I am lifted and gifted. I am blessed and helped. Devil, you are in store for a surprise. I no longer belong in your clan of puppets. The Lord has set me free, I AM FREE INDEED, FREE TO DANCE, FREE TO SING AND FREE TO WORSHIP MY SAVIOR, JESUS CHRIST, Amen Hallelujah.

SCRIPTURES

Psalm 107:2
2 Let the redeemed of the LORD say so, whom he hath redeemed from the hand of the enemy.

I Corinthians 15:54
54 So when this corruptible shall have put on incorruption, and this mortal shall have put on immortality, then shall be brought to pass the saying that is written, Death is swallowed up in victory.

***Revelation 4:1-11** (Heavenly Worship)*

DAY NINETEEN

Healed and Comforted

TODAY I decree and declare that there is a great release upon my life to conceive and birth great things. God is dealing with me favorably and I am not denied. My better days are here. My health is made perfect to give me rest of mind. No

hiding agent of death is allowed inside my body. I am fully healed and comforted. My reproach is cancelled. I am a new identity of honor. I command every form of lack to disappear and never to re-appear. My soul shall magnify the Lord over my petitions. The generations of the upright shall call me blessed. Neighbors will rejoice with me. My blessings will span from coast to coast. I am becoming mighty, for the Lord's mercy is being poured out for my sake. I am cladded in the garment of royalty. Divine royalty is erasing my areas of inferiorities. I have a new robe of respect. God is filling me up with amazing grace. This is my year of Amazing Heights. I am being empowered to prosper. Every hindrance is being removed. No more stumbling blocks. I have stepping stones. I am reaching desired mile markers and excelling in expectations. I declare these things and I believe I have them, in the name of Jesus Christ, Amen.

SCRIPTURES

Luke 1:23-58 (Birth of Jesus' Foretold)

THE YOKE BREAKER

DAY TWENTY

Rejoicing in the Savior

IN the name of Jesus Christ, I decree and declare that the Lord remembers me today, and I am not hindered to prosper. The Lord is sending a fresh word to me. It shall be a word of healing, prosperity and love. His word shall prosper me, as it would not return void. My soul shall magnify the Lord over my petitions. I will forever rejoice in my Savior. I am protected from people stronger than me. I shall conceive and not abort my expectations. The God who answered Hannah is on my side. My prayers shall be granted. I am being jet propelled into heights uncommon. I shall remain sustained. I have limitless advancement and my success shall remain unending. This day will bless me more than yesterday. Tomorrow shall be better than today, as I go from glory to glory. My Lord has accelerated me. I am way ahead of the enemies. I and my loved ones shall not end in shallow graves. Our lives shall not be cut short by arrows of hate. I am in God's good book, my portion is preserved, in the name of Jesus Christ, Amen.

SCRIPTURES

Isaiah 55:11
11 So shall my word be that goeth forth out of my mouth: it shall not return unto me void, but it shall accomplish that which I please, and it shall prosper in the thing whereto I sent it.

1 Samuel 1:27
27 For this child I prayed; and the LORD hath given me my petition which I asked of him:

Isaiah 59:14-16 (Advice against Sin)

DAY TWENTY ONE

Peace from Adversaries

IN the name of Jesus Christ, today I command everlasting happiness over me and my loved ones. I command perpetual shame over my adversaries. I command Heaven to open its abundance of grace upon me. I command the earth to swallow evil messengers who are after my peace. I command the increase of the earth to be to my favor. I command deficits over the efforts of those after my goodness. I command the Holy Spirit to fight my battle. I command the Holy Spirit to fight against my enemies. I command fire over the meetings of those plotting my fall. I command an uplifting upon every move I am making to succeed. I decree success, I receive success. I decree happiness; I receive happiness. I call forth unending supplies, I receive them from the throne of mercy. My expectations shall end well. I am not broke and will never be broke. I am not forgotten and will never be forgotten by God. My days are brighter. My hope is built in Christ, My joy remains intact. I have comfort on every side. My portion is protected. I am the beloved of the Lord, chosen to rise and shine, in the name of Jesus Christ, Amen.

SCRIPTURES

Isaiah 60:1
1 Arise, shine; for thy light is come, and the glory of the LORD is risen upon thee.

Isaiah 61:1-3 *(Good Tiding of Salvation)*

Psalm 1:1*-end (The Way of the Righteous)*

DAY TWENTY TWO

I'm Strong and Relevant

TODAY I declare, whether the devil likes it or not, I am being rewarded. There shall be great celebrations over me. My health and wealth are becoming massively amazing.

Diverse blessings are poured over me. I am a recipient of rain and riches. I am a recipient of honor and favor. I am a recipient of promotion and advancement. I am a recipient of divine freedom; therefore, no chain is holding me down. The hands of the Lord has established me; therefore, I shall not end up hopeless in any situation. The power of the Lord is upon me, I shall not be weary or faint. I am not in the fold of the rejected. I have been called and favored by divine grace. I have all surplus. I have all happiness. I have all peace. I have all freedom. I have all spiritual empowerment. I have the fullness of joy. I shall make devil mad every day. He is a defeated coward. I have power for exploits, I am unshakable and indefatigable. I am strong and relevant for these days. Nations and kings shall seek my counsel. I have excellent spirit. I am being propelled into amazing heights. I declare these things, and they are settled, in the name of Jesus Christ, Amen.

SCRIPTURES

Psalm 89:21
21 With whom my hand shall be established: mine arm also shall strengthen him.

Isaiah 40:31
31 But they that wait upon the LORD shall renew their strength; they shall mount up with wings as eagles; they shall run, and not be weary; and they shall walk, and not faint.

DAY TWENTY THREE

Divine Protection

TODAY I come in the name of Jesus Christ, and decree over me and my household, that we are focused and not fatigued. I command bones to have flesh and be energized. I command blood to become pure, and not afflicted by agents

of death. I command veins to be renewed and very functional. I command kidneys to function to perfection. I command livers to work right and deliver necessary assistance to vital areas. I command the brain to align with the mind as both remain under divine instruction. I command flesh to become impermeable for the antics and attacks of demonic forces. I command eyes healed of any agent of blindness. I command spiritual blindness healed. I command lust away from the eyes of Believers. I command the mind to function as desired by the Lord, Jesus. I command legs to be ordered by the spirit of the Lord. I command hands to desire sacred things. I command virtues protected and preserved. I command divine protection over me and my family. Nothing missing, nothing in a shambles, in the name of Jesus Christ, Amen.

SCRIPTURES

Job 22:28
28 Thou shalt also decree a thing, and it shall be established unto thee: and the light shall shine upon thy ways.

Jeremiah 33:6
6 Behold, I will bring it health and cure, and I will cure them, and will reveal unto them the abundance of peace and truth.

DAY TWENTY FOUR

Living in Divine Affluence

TODAY I come in the name of Jesus Christ to decree and declare that I am having a marvelous outing. My prayers are blessed and shall not return unanswered. Long-awaited expectations are manifesting. The Yoke Breaker is leading me this day. I am ending big time. The Way Maker is leading my path; therefore, my success is sure and settled. The Unshakable Shaker is leading my battle; therefore, nothing shall put me to flight. My God is greater than my confrontations. I shall win in a grand style. My God is bigger than the opposition. I shall subdue the enemies. My Creator is the master over the universe. I have His permission to prosper, and nothing is able to stop me. I am getting much better. I am living in divine affluence. I am nourished and spiritually pampered. Favor stays in my direction. Money loves my home. Perfect health is my reward of worship. I have my desires. I have a beautiful heritage. This day is ending for me on a note of jubilation. I am being approved and honored. This is my day, and it shall remain as decreed in the name of Jesus Christ, Amen.

SCRIPTURES

Psalm 16 *(Joy in God's Presence)*

DAY TWENTY FIVE

Affirming Salvation

IN the name of Jesus Christ, this is my day to rejoice over my portion, and to celebrate over the demise of my enemies. In the Book of Psalms Chapter 118:14 says, "The LORD is my strength and song, and is become my salvation"; therefore, I decree and declare that the power of the Lord is moving me from victory to victory. My song shall ever be the song of rejoicing. My salvation is affirmed by the blood of Jesus, I am preserved, protected and sanctified. I shall not die but live and declare the works of the Lord. The gates of righteousness are opened unto me, I have access to the abundance of Heaven. I have become relevant from this day, to enter into greater territories and rule. I shall not be subdued. I shall not serve my peers. Any plot against my goodness and peace shall attract the wrath of God. My enemies shall wither and perish. The sea shall open its mouth and swallow those pursuing my destiny. Where I have been rejected, I am becoming the mighty corner stone. The Lord is sending my prosperity today. All my needs are met. All my purposes are fulfilled. The bountiful kindness of the Lord is toward me and my household. I have trusted in the Lord; therefore, I will remain as Mount Zion, which cannot be removed, but abides forever. I pray favor to locate me today. I pray mercies to locate my fingers. I pray joy to fill my heart. I am moving into great supernatural increase. This is my portion. This is the will and purpose of the Lord for me. This is my day. I shall be glad and not return sad, in the name of Jesus Christ, Amen.

SCRIPTURES

Psalm 118 *(The LORD'S Mercy)*

Psalm 125 *(The LORD the Protector)*

THE YOKE BREAKER

DAY TWENTY SIX

God's Favor is Upon Me

TODAY I decree and declare that I will not suffer, and I will not be chained down by evil forces. Jonathan stood for David in 1 Samuel 19:4, and David escaped his arch enemy. I decree that the enemy of my soul shall fail. Members of their household will become their enemies. They shall not speak with one voice. The counsel of the ungodly shall perish, and I will receive favor from unusual quarters. The favor of the Lord is upon me. I will meander through the camps of the enemies, and they shall not be able to raise a finger. Today I become unreachable for killers and rapists. Today I become a commander over the camps of the enemy. Today the words of my mouth shall rule the territories around me. By the power of the Lord, I am controlling business deals. By the spirit of the Lord, I am determining wealth transfers. Global recession has no power over my provision. The Lord has spoken concerning my portion. My barrel of meal shall not waste, neither shall the cruse of oil fail in my home. Every agent of envy in my path is hereby evicted from the land of grace. They shall eat and drink their own blood. As for me, the goodness of the Lord is locating me daily. Everything the enemy has removed is relocating to find me and settle in my bosom permanently. My days of wrestling with poverty are over. My days of basking in super abundance are here. I have the Lord on my side, I shall live and not die, to proclaim the wonderful works of my God. I declare these things, and they shall be as declared in the name of Jesus Christ, Amen.

SCRIPTURES

1 Kings 17 *(The Lord Your Provider)*

Genesis 30 *(The Sons of Jacob)*

DAY TWENTY SEVEN

Boldness in the Spirit

THIS day, I am advancing by new identity, and fresh unction. I am being transformed from a sinner to a giant. The mighty valor inside of me is getting discovered. The best days of my life are before me. I am approved to attack and subdue.

I am empowered to command over territories. Where I have been used, I will start ruling from today. Where they used me as the cleaner, I am becoming the owner. Grace and unstoppable power are over me to demand and receive. My beauty is coming alive and shining brighter. I shall not die as a nonentity. I belong to the family of champions. I have been authorized from birth to live in divine affluence. Nothing shall be able to stop me. Courage is alive inside of me. Boldness is made available in my spirit. The Lord has favored my purpose. He has declared my best days. I shall fear no evil, for the Lord is with me. I am approved for better days and seasons of joy. My focus is firm. My destiny is favorable. I have faced grim adversities, but right now, no giant shall be too great for my anointing. Today my giants are falling. Today my greatness is rising. I am of the Lord who saves not by sword and spear, the battle before me is not mine but belongs to my God. I declare victory over obstacles and doubts. Victory is mine in the name of Jesus Christ, Amen.

SCRIPTURES

1 Samuel 17: 37, 47
37 David said moreover, The LORD that delivered me out of the paw of the lion, and out of the paw of the bear, he will deliver me out of the hand of this Philistine. And Saul said unto David, Go, and the LORD be with thee.

47 And all this assembly shall know that the LORD saveth not with sword and spear: for the battle is the LORD's, and he will give you into our hands.

Judges 6 *(Gideon becomes Israel's Judge)*

DAY TWENTY EIGHT

Deliverance from Transgressions

TODAY I raise the banner of glory and perfection. I shall not be ashamed. The Lord is my Deliverer. He has delivered me from my transgressions. I shall never be the reproach of the foolish. I am recovering from past confrontations of the enemy. The Lord has spared my life My health has recovered. In my season, the Lord has made all things beautiful; therefore, I have the assurance of beauty for ashes. I am for signs and wonders. The plot of the enemy is come to nought. It shall not stand, for the Lord is with me. Every yoke of burden against me is broken; therefore, I have the joy of harvest in my spirit. The Lord has borne my griefs. I am protected from sorrow. The Lord has commanded great grace over me; therefore, I shall no more be termed forsaken, neither shall my land any more be termed desolate, but I shall be called Hephzibah, and my land Beulah; for the Lord delights in me and my land shall be married. All the works of my hands shall give me joy. I have excellence if every area of my life. I am winning forever, in the name of Jesus Christ, Amen.

SCRIPTURES

Psalm 39:8
8 Deliver me from all my transgressions: make me not the reproach of the foolish.

Isaiah 53:4
4 Surely he hath borne our griefs, and carried our sorrows: yet we did esteem him stricken, smitten of God, and afflicted.

Isaiah 62:4
4 Thou shalt no more be termed Forsaken; neither shall thy land any more be termed Desolate: but thou shalt be called Hephzibah, and thy land Beulah: for the LORD delighteth in thee, and thy land shall be married.

Isaiah 8:10, 18 (Coming of the Deliverer)

THE YOKE BREAKER

DAY TWENTY NINE

Basking in Everlasting Peace

TODAY I bask in the covenant of peace. It is an everlasting peace for me and my generations. The Lord is multiplying us and placing us under amazing conditions. I am becoming a permanent sanctuary of the Lord and His tabernacle shall

be with me forever. This is the season of change. I declare things to change to my delight. The Lord's decree is ruling over human accusations against me. The world shall know that I have a God who rules in the kingdom of men and has the power to enthrone and dethrone. My answer is released for my promotion. I nullify the antics of the prince of the kingdom of Persia. Nothing is delayed any longer. The divine lifter of my head is released to help me. My days are getting better. My health is renewed and preserved. I am receiving my letters of joy. My loved ones are coming closer. My financial situation is getting brighter. I decree permanent extinction to poverty and disappointment in my generation. This is the day of the Lord. I will go in courage, and I shall return with the songs of victories. I pray these desires, and they shall appear in the name of Jesus Christ, Amen.

SCRIPTURES

Ezekiel 37: 26-27
26 Moreover I will make a covenant of peace with them; it shall be an everlasting covenant with them: and I will place them, and multiply them, and will set my sanctuary in the midst of them for evermore.

27 My tabernacle also shall be with them: yea, I will be their God, and they shall be my people.

Daniel 10: 12-20 *(Daniel's Vision of an Angel)*

DAY THIRTY

Preserved and Protected

TODAY I speak against the gates of hell. they shall not prevail over my ambitions. I receive the spirit of knowledge. I will discern the things of God and live according to His purpose. The bright clouds of salvation are over me and my household. We are preserved and protected. The

Lord has declared me as His beloved. The whole world shall listen and respect me. I have power and authority over devils and to cure diseases; therefore, I bind cancer and other forms of deadly diseases. I bind poverty and barrenness. I bind evil penetrations and insinuations of the enemy. I bind the mouth of witches and wizards.

I bind the spirit of hate and low self-esteem. I bind every concocted attack against the Believers. I bind the enemy of peace and freedom. I bind wayward attractions to same sex. I bind the spirit of disunity and gossip. I bind the agents of embezzlement. I bind the spirit of pride and lust for ill-gotten wealth. I bind territorial demons. I bind the visitations of spirit husbands and wives. I bind demonic rapists. I bind the mouths of the agents of lesser gods. I bind the spirit of insatiable sex and alcoholism. I bind these spirits and their father, the devil. In the name of Jesus Christ, I release favor and the knowledge of God almighty in my direction. I release perfection and redemption. I release divine increase and supernatural maturity. I release the greatness of the kingdom of God. I call forth blessings uncommon and unending. I call forth power and productivity. I decree and declare that the spirit of the Lord God is upon me; therefore, I will rise and shine, in the name of Jesus Christ, Amen.

SCRIPTURES

Matthew 16:18
18 And I say also unto thee, That thou art Peter, and upon this rock I will build my church; and the gates of hell shall not prevail against it.

Matthew 17:5
5 While he yet spake, behold, a bright cloud overshadowed them: and behold a voice out of the cloud, which said, This is my beloved Son, in whom I am well pleased; hear ye him.

Isaiah 61: 1-7 (Good Tidings of Salvation)

THE YOKE BREAKER

DAY THIRTY ONE

God's Faithfulness

TODAY I release the abundance of Heaven over me and my household. I have my desires fulfilled, and I am ending this month fulfilled. I have no regrets, for my faith is firm and steady. The Lord shall complete what He started. He has begun a good work in me, and He is a faithful God. I have not been denied, and I will never be denied. I am not rejected, and I will never be rejected. Disappointments are not my portion. I am thriving, not begging. I am looking forward to a brighter new month and I am sure it will be more rewarding. I am having double for my trouble. Everlasting joy is my prize. Good tidings are filling my days. I remain faithful, and it shall be counted as righteousness for me. By grace, I will achieve lofty gains. The word of the Lord shall profit me daily. I will not miss Heaven. I will not miss mansions prepared for me by Jesus Christ. Every plot to pluck me off the street is turned back to the plotters and their parents. I am guarded and guided by the Holy Spirit. My days are brighter; my life is safe and sound. Jesus is my lover, I rest in His love. I declare these things, and they are settled in the name of Jesus Christ, Amen.

SCRIPTURES

Hebrews 4 *(The Promise of Rest)*
1 Let us therefore fear, lest, a promise being left us of entering into his rest, any of you should seem to come short of it. ...

Isaiah 61: 1-7 *(Good Tidings of Salvation)*

THE AUTHOR
DR. EMMANUEL ROTIMI ONABANJO

www.paeministry.org

Dr. Emmanuel Rotimi Onabanjo is the Senior Pastor of Power and Authority Evangelical Ministry, headquartered in the New York City borough of Brooklyn, with branches in West Palm Beach, Florida; Lagos, Nigeria; and Chennai, India. Dr. Onabanjo also heads The Yoke Breaker, a global Prophetic and Deliverance Revival Outreach, which operates in several parts of the United States, Nigeria, South Africa, United Kingdom, Ireland and India. The Yoke Breaker also features a daily radio prayer program that airs Mondays through Fridays on New York's most popular gospel radio station, WLIB 1190 AM, at 5:30 a.m.

Dr. Onabanjo, a journalism graduate from Ogun State Polytechnic, now known as Moshood Abiola Polytechnic, served as an editor at the Daily Sketch, a national newspaper in Nigeria, before he relocated to the U.S. in the mid-1990s. Dr. Onabanjo, who also earned a master's degree in divinity and a Ph.D. in pastoral ministries in Indiana, USA, is a servant of God, blessed with the gifts of prophecy and healing.

In 2015, Dr. Onabanjo was appointed to Brooklyn's clergy advisory board by the borough's president. Additionally, Dr. Onabanjo serves as Dean of Studies for the Bill Winston's School of Ministry's satellite campus in New York. He is the proud husband of First Lady Margaret Onabanjo, who works alongside him in the Ministry, and together, they are raising two children, Oluwaseun and Olaoluwa.

PAE Ministries
889 Sheffield Avenue
Brooklyn, NY 11207, USA
(718) 290-4040

THE YOKE BREAKER

NOTE

www.ingramcontent.com/pod-product-compliance
Lightning Source LLC
Chambersburg PA
CBHW070048070426
42449CB00012BA/3191

* 9 7 8 0 9 9 8 2 0 4 0 2 4 *